A Mo

The place was Joe Robbie Stadium in Miami. The day was January 22, 1989. The game was the Super Bowl. And the man of the moment was Jerry Rice, wide receiver for the San Francisco 49ers.

This was Jerry's fourth season in the National Football League, and his first Super Bowl. And here he was, nursing an ankle injured only six days before the biggest game of his career.

With only 3 minutes and 10 seconds left to play, and the Cincinnati Bengals leading 16–13, Jerry ignored the ankle pain as he trotted onto the field. In the huddle, he could see that many of his teammates were worried. "Let's go, be tough," 49ers quarterback Joe Montana said. Jerry knew all about being tough.

Here are all the details of one of the most exciting last-minute victories in Super Bowl history, focused on the man who would be named Most Valuable Player. How did he get this good? How does he stay this good? Who influenced his life on and off the field? All the answers, and more, are in the pages of this *Sports Illustrated for Kids* book, JERRY RICE.

Jerry Rice

By John Rolfe

Illustrated by Steve McGarry

A Sports Illustrated for Kids Book

Bantam Books
Toronto • New York • London • Sydney • Auckland

JERRY RICE
A Bantam Book/November 1993

SPORTS ILLUSTRATED FOR KIDS and
are trademarks of Time Inc.
SPORTS ILLUSTRATED FOR KIDS BOOKS® is an imprint of
Bantam Doubleday Dell Publishing Group, Inc.
All rights reserved. Used under authorization.

Cover design by Miriam Dustin
Cover photograph by Peter Read Miller
Interior illustrations by Steve McGarry

ISBN 0-553-48157-6

Published simultaneously in the United States and Canada.

PRINTED IN THE UNITED STATES OF AMERICA

0 9 8 7 6 5 4 3 2 1
CWO

This book is dedicated to my father, Raymond Rolfe, who has given me the gifts of love, laughter, an appreciation of sports, and the knowledge that few things in life are as important as education.

Special thanks to my wife, Victoria, for keeping the home fires burning, and to my editor, Margaret Sieck (And Ye Shall Find), for her patience and guidance.

Contents

Super Bowl of Rice

San Francisco 49ers wide receiver Jerry Rice was on a mission when his team played the Cincinnati Bengals in Super Bowl XXIII on January 22, 1989, in Miami, Florida.

During his first three seasons in the National Football League (NFL), from 1985 through 1987, Jerry had earned several honors. He had been named the National Football Conference (NFC) Rookie of the Year in 1985 and the league's Most Valuable Player in 1987. But during that time, he failed to catch a single touchdown pass in any of the 49ers' playoff games. As a result, some people wondered if he deserved his reputation as the best wide receiver in pro football.

Jerry's fourth season, 1988, had been frustrating. He injured his right ankle in a game in October and ended up catching 64 passes for 1,306 yards and only 9 touchdowns for the season. Most receivers would be delighted with those totals. By Jerry's standards, they were disappointing. So when the 49ers entered the playoffs in January 1989, a big question had still not been answered: would Jerry ever live up to his reputation in a big game?

Jerry came back with the answer. He caught a total of five touchdown passes in playoff wins over the Minnesota Vikings and Chicago Bears. And that wasn't all. When the 49ers met the Bengals in the Super Bowl, he wanted to show he could do even more. After all, the Super Bowl is the biggest football game there is. He would be playing in front of a sellout crowd of 75,129 fans in Miami's Joe Robbie Stadium, with millions more watching on TV.

At first, it looked as though Jerry would not get a chance to prove himself. He twisted his right ankle in practice six days before the game. The 49ers were afraid that he would be unable to play. Jerry made up his mind that there was no way he was going to miss his first Super Bowl. "This has been my ultimate dream," he told reporters before the game. "I'm not going to let my ankle get me down. I might not be 100 percent, but I'll be there."

The first half of the game was a brutal defensive battle. On only the third play, 49ers left tackle Steve Wallace broke his left ankle. Several minutes later, Bengals nose guard Tim Krumrie fell to the ground with a shattered left leg, the result of a wrenching fall. Joe Montana, the 49ers' quarterback, was pounced on by Bengal pass rushers who sacked him twice and forced him to fumble once, although he was able to recover the fumble.

Cincinnati's defense was confident it could stop Jerry. Sometimes two defensive backs covered him. Other times, a single back would try to bump him and knock him off his stride as he started running his pass routes. (These are the planned paths receivers take to get into position to catch the ball.) Jerry, however, was happy to find that his ankle could support the quick moves he needed to get away from defenders.

Jerry's first catch of the game gained 12 yards during a drive that led to a San Francisco field goal in the first quarter. He later made a nifty one-handed grab of a pass that seemed to be three or four feet beyond his reach. When the pass arrived, he reached up, tipped the ball, and grabbed it for a 16-yard gain. Three plays later, he snared a pass for a 30-yard gain, but the 49ers didn't score on that drive. The first half ended with the teams tied, 3–3.

In the third quarter, each team scored another field goal. Cincinnati then went ahead after running the ball back 93 yards for a touchdown. The Bengals led, 13–6.

With only 34 seconds left in the third quarter, San Francisco began a drive that ended with Jerry scoring a touchdown to tie the game. On the 49ers' first play of the drive, Jerry caught a pass, shook off a tackle, and gained 31 yards. After San Francisco had reached the Bengals' 14-yard line, Joe Montana lofted the ball and Jerry caught it over his shoulder on the 5-yard line. Jerry's momentum started to carry him out of bounds, but he twisted his body and was just able to get the ball into the end zone. The referee raised his arms over his head. Touchdown! The score was tied again.

The next time the 49ers got the ball, Joe Montana heaved a pass deep downfield. Jerry was racing along with Bengal defensive back Lewis Billups right beside him. Jerry slowed a bit and nudged Lewis away. Then Jerry leaped and made a diving catch for a 44-yard gain.

Jerry felt pain shoot through his ankle when he hit the ground after the catch. He got up and limped off the field. The 49ers' trainer wrapped tape around Jerry's ankle while Jerry sat on the bench and watched his teammates try for a field goal. Unfortunately, placekicker Mike Cofer missed the field goal.

The Bengals took over the ball on their own 32-yard line. Jerry watched from the sideline as they drove up the field and kicked a field goal that gave them a 16–13 lead. When the Niners got the ball back, there were only 3 minutes and 10 seconds left to play and they were on their own 8-yard line. They needed to gain at least 60 yards before they would be close enough for their placekicker to try for the tying field goal.

Jerry ignored the pain in his ankle as he trotted onto the field. In the huddle, he could see that many of his teammates were very worried. They looked as if they were about to go to war. "Let's go, be tough," Joe Montana said.

Using short passes and running plays, the 49ers began to drive down the field. With a little more than one minute left in the game, the 49ers were on the Bengals' 45-yard line—still out of field goal range. They needed a big play.

When the ball was snapped, Jerry raced downfield and cut across the middle. He was surrounded by three defensive backs whose job it was to keep Jerry from catching the ball. Joe Montana fired the ball anyway, and Jerry made what one Bengal later called "a perfect catch." With the ball in hand, he burst away from the defenders and sprinted to the 18-yard line before he was tackled. He had gained 27 yards! The 49ers were close enough to kick a field goal and tie the game, but they decided to try for the game-winning touchdown instead.

Then, with only 39 seconds left, the crowd was roaring as Jerry lined up near the right sideline. As Joe Montana barked out his signals, Jerry went into action. He ran straight across the field to the left side, near where wide receiver John Taylor was standing. When the ball was snapped, Jerry and John ran into the end zone. Bengal defensive back Ray Horton was supposed

What's in a Name?
The San Francisco 49ers are named after the pioneers who settled in Northern California after gold was discovered there in 1849. Many of those pioneers helped build the city of San Francisco. The team's official colors are gold and scarlet.

to cover John, but he froze for a second when he saw Jerry coming at him. Which one should he cover? That pause gave John just enough time to get open by a step.

Joe threw. Ray dove for the ball. John made the catch. Touchdown! The crowd exploded with cheers. San Francisco won, 20–16. It was one of the most exciting finishes in Super Bowl history.

Jerry was named the game's Most Valuable Player. He had caught 11 passes for a Super Bowl record total of 215 yards. "I did okay," he said as he accepted the MVP trophy in the locker room after the game. "If it was up to me, I would have given the MVP to Joe Montana. He took control and gave the leadership we needed. I'm a modest guy. I don't like to take credit."

There was plenty of credit for Jerry to take. "He was playing on guts," 49ers running back Roger Craig said. "He was hurting. But if there is a war breaking out, you can count on him being ready for it."

"Going into this game, I was so motivated," Jerry explained. "I just wanted to win so badly. It's not often that you have an opportunity to play in the Super Bowl."

In the Cincinnati locker room, the Bengals were shaking their heads in amazement. "What else can you say but accept the truth?" asked linebacker Reggie Williams. "Jerry Rice is one of the more phenomenal athletes in the league. No doubt about it."

Bengal defensive back Eric Thomas said, "I didn't think anybody could make the plays on us that Jerry Rice did. He was making plays that I've never seen."

Jerry's teammates weren't surprised. "I've said all along that Jerry Rice is the best wide receiver ever to play this game," said 49ers defensive back Ronnie Lott. "Yes, ever."

Since that Super Bowl, it has been hard to find anyone who disagrees. From 1985 through 1992, Jerry was named All-Pro at his position six times. That means that sportswriters placed him on the list of the year's best players. He has been named to play in the Pro Bowl seven times by his fellow players. He has caught more touchdown passes than anyone in NFL history. After the 1992 season, he had caught 103. In 1987, he set a single-season NFL record with 22 touchdown catches. He holds the NFL record for most touchdown catches in post-season play (13). He is also one of only nine pro receivers ever to gain more than 10,000 yards during a career.

There are many reasons why Jerry is so great. He has big, soft, strong hands that help him grab and hold on to the ball. He has the ability to concentrate in tense situations or when he is hurt. At 6'2", he is tall for a wide receiver, and he can leap high enough to dunk a basketball. He isn't the fastest receiver in the NFL, but he makes up for it by being smart. "Jerry has a knack of

Jerry's Favorite Things

Food:	Pasta, fish
Color:	49er Red
Hobby:	Listening to music
Cars:	Porsche, Mercedes
Number:	80
Sport to Watch (other than football):	Basketball
Sport to Play (other than football):	Basketball
Athletes:	Will Clark and Lynn Swann
Biggest Sports Thrill:	Being named Most Valuable Player of the 1989 Super Bowl

knowing just when to use his speed," says Joe Montana. "He uses just enough speed to get open and has enough left when he gets to the ball."

"Jerry's got game speed," adds Ronnie Lott. "It's hard to explain. He may run a 40-yard dash in 4.5 or 4.6 seconds [really fast receivers run it in 4.2 seconds], but on game day, nobody catches him."

Jerry is also a master at outsmarting defenders. "I like the defender to think the opposite of what I'm going to do," he says. He studies defenses closely and usually knows what they are going to do before the ball is snapped. That gives him a big advantage.

Most of all, Jerry is always willing to practice and work as hard as he can to make the most of his talent. Many players take time off after a season to relax. Jerry begins a tough daily workout routine right away so that he will stay in top physical shape.

Talent, smarts, and a willingness to work hard: when you add them all up, you get a future NFL Hall of Famer. Or as 49ers defensive back Tim McKyer once said, "You feed all the data of the ideal receiver into a computer and it spits out Jerry Rice."

Brick by Brick

Jerry Lee Rice was born on October 13, 1962, in Starkville, Mississippi. He is the sixth of eight kids. He has two sisters, Eddie and Loistine, and five brothers: Joe, Tom, James, Jimmy, and Zebedee.

Jerry and his family lived in the town of Crawford, which is 38 miles southeast of Starkville. About 500 people lived in the tiny community surrounded by farms and countryside. A 40-foot-long trailer served as Crawford's town hall, public library, and fire department headquarters. There were no sidewalks, streetlights, or traffic signs.

The house that Jerry lived in while he was growing up had been built by his dad, Joe Nathan Rice. Mr. Rice was a bricklayer who worked on local construction projects. The Rice family lived comfortably, but they didn't have a lot of money. "We had to wait our turn for things like clothes and shoes," Jerry says. "We had discipline and plenty of it."

Jerry was a happy, carefree kid. "He never gave anyone any trouble," says his mom, Eddie B. Rice. "He was always quiet, but he loved his ballplaying."

Basketball and football were Jerry's favorite sports when he was growing up. During the football season, he and his brothers watched Dallas Cowboys games on TV. Jerry's favorite player was a wide receiver named Drew Pearson who played for the Cowboys from 1973 to 1983. "When I was real young, I always thought about either playing for Dallas or against them," Jerry says.

Having five brothers meant Jerry always had someone to play with or against. When they weren't throw-

Time Capsule

In 1972, the year Jerry turned 10 years old:

*The Dallas Cowboys beat the Miami Dolphins, 24–3, in the Super Bowl.

*Eleven Israeli athletes were murdered by Palestinian terrorists at the Summer Olympic Games in Munich, Germany.

*Astronauts walked on the moon (and haven't since!).

*The Godfather won the Academy Award for Best Picture.

ing a football around or shooting baskets, Jerry and his brothers liked to chase and ride their neighbors' horses. There was a big field behind the Rices' house where the horses grazed. "The horses didn't just come to you," Jerry says. "If you wanted to ride, you chased them down."

Jerry believes that a number of things he did as a kid helped him develop as a football player. One of those things was chasing down the horses. Those chases made him learn how to change direction quickly while running. This skill is useful on the football field when a player has to avoid defenders in order to catch a pass. Jerry later built his staying power by often running to and from high school, which was five miles from his house. "You know, that's what made me," Jerry says, "running those back dirt roads and country fields."

There was another activity that played an important role in turning Jerry into a great receiver: working with bricks. During summers when he was a teenager, Jerry helped his dad at work. From eight o'clock in the morning until five in the evening, Jerry pushed wheelbarrows full of cement. He also caught bricks tossed to him by his brothers Tom, James, and Jimmy. After he caught them, he would pile them up next to where their father was working.

"I was on this tall scaffold [a type of platform] and they'd toss the bricks up to me," Jerry says. "I was catching bricks all day. One of my brothers would stack up four and throw them. The bricks might go this way and that, and I would catch all four."

Catching bricks stretched Jerry's hands and made them strong. It also made his hand-to-eye coordination so sharp that he could catch almost anything that was thrown to him.

Mr. Rice was impressed by Jerry's work habits. "He handled bricks better than any worker I ever had," he says.

It wasn't an easy job. Jerry spent many days working under a hot sun when the temperature was around 100 degrees. "It really made me a better person," he says. "I knew what hard work was all about."

Working with his dad made Jerry think about what he wanted to do when he grew up. One thing was certain: he did not want to spend the rest of his life as a bricklayer. He liked working with his hands, though. One of his hobbies was fixing broken appliances and toys. "I always had a special touch with my hands," he says. "I thought I'd be doing something like electronics or repairing things. I wanted to open my own shop someday."

Jerry never thought seriously about a career in professional sports, even though he was a good athlete. He averaged 30 points a game as a forward on the basketball team at B. L. Moor High School in Crawford. He competed as a high jumper on the school's track team.

Football, however, was something he had lost interest in. "I liked basketball·better," he says. "I never thought of football as anything I would do for a living. I never thought of it as my future. I had no intention of playing football."

That changed one day during Jerry's sophomore year in high school. Jerry was cutting a class when the vice principal spotted him standing in the hallway. The vice principal walked up behind him and tapped him on the shoulder. Jerry turned around, took one look at who it was, and darted around the corner in a flash. The vice principal ran after him. When he caught up, he told Jerry, "The football team could use someone with your speed."

Jerry was given a choice: try out for the football team or be punished with detention. Jerry chose football and his life was changed forever. When he tried out for the team and found that he was good at catching passes, he thought football might be fun again.

Jerry's dad remembers when he noticed that Jerry had a special talent in football. "I saw him dive in a thorn bush after a ball one day," says Mr. Rice. "He got stuck bad, but he caught it. When I saw that, I felt something."

Mrs. Rice didn't like the idea of Jerry playing football. She was worried that he would get injured. "But the more I fought it, the more determined he was, so I gave it up," she says.

Jerry's speed was put to use on offense, where he was a receiver. Jerry turned out to be a very good wide receiver. He caught 35 touchdown passes during his senior season in 1980.

Jerry hoped that his success in high school would help him win a football scholarship to college. Unfortunately, he received only a few scholarship offers. Many college recruiters thought Jerry lacked experience because he had played only two years of high school football instead of three or four. Others, believe it or not, thought he was too slow. They did not understand that he might not run very fast for a measured distance, but he had a talent for using his speed well in games. "This is not a track meet, it's football," Jerry says. "I really don't think you have to be that fast. It's how you run your routes."

Only one college, Mississippi Valley State University (called Valley), bothered to send its head coach to watch Jerry play. When Coach Archie Cooley saw Jerry for the first time, he knew why so many recruiters weren't interested. "Jerry was about 6'1", 180 pounds and ran the 40-yard dash in about 4.8 seconds," Coach Cooley says. "You could find that kind of player any-where, but he had those hands and he had the desire to improve."

Coach Cooley offered Jerry a scholarship, but Jerry wasn't thrilled. Valley is a tiny school with just 2,600 students. It does not have a big-time football program.

The State of Mississippi

Jerry's home state gets its name from the Mississippi River, the longest river in the United States. It flows 2,348 miles from Minnesota south to the Gulf of Mexico. In 1817, Mississippi became America's 20th state. Other famous people from Mississippi are music legend Elvis Presley, talk show host Oprah Winfrey, and Muppet creator Jim Henson.

It does not play against powerhouse opponents like the University of Nebraska or Michigan. Valley is only a Division I-AA school. Jerry would have preferred a school in Division I-A, the highest level of college sports.

One thing about playing at a small school is that most of the school's games are not covered by national magazines, newspapers, and TV. Jerry had almost no chance of getting enough national attention to catch the eye of scouts who work for pro football teams. In the end, however, he agreed to go to Valley because his brother, Tom, talked him into it.

Tom Rice had played football at Jackson State University in Jackson, Mississippi. Jackson State played Mississippi Valley State each year, and Tom had seen that Valley's teams loved to pass. He knew Valley would be a good place for Jerry to continue developing his receiving skills.

There was one other thing that convinced Jerry to go. It was a dream that Tom and Jerry shared about what they would do if they ever became famous athletes. "Both of us talked about one day building a house for our parents," Jerry says. Tom did not go on to have a pro career after college. "I was the last hope," says Jerry.

In 1981, when Jerry left for college, it did not seem likely that he would be able to fulfill that dream. Then again, as Jerry's mom says, "You just never know what God has in the storehouse for you."

In Jerry's case, the storehouse was full of touchdown catches and receiving records.

World, Satellite, and the Gunslinger

Going away to college was easy for Jerry. For one thing, he wasn't very far from home. Mississippi Valley State University is about 100 miles west of Crawford in the town of Itta Bena. There are only about 2,600 students at Valley and another 2,900 people living in Itta Bena, so life for him there was almost as quiet and simple as it had been back home.

Jerry lived in a dormitory on the university campus. There, he became known for a trait he still has today: neatness. "In high school, my room was a mess," he says. "Everything everywhere, clothes everywhere. My whole life-style changed in college. My roommate was a real messy type and I had to pick up behind him. I wanted to be neat. I liked to be in a clean atmosphere so I could relax."

Jerry studied auto mechanics, and health and physical education. Tinkering with cars was fun because it allowed him to work with his hands. Of course, he also got a chance to use those hands on the football field.

Jerry's freshman season with the Mississippi Valley Delta Devils was promising enough. He caught 30 passes for 432 yards and 2 touchdowns. Those were modest totals, but Coach Cooley was pleased. He could see that Jerry had the potential to do much, much more.

Coach Cooley demanded the best from his players. Jerry showed he could work hard at football. "My work ethic when I came to the 49ers, I had it because Coach Cooley really worked me hard," he says. "He got me prepared for the NFL."

After the season, Jerry started lifting weights and running sprints. He became stronger and quicker. It paid off during his sophomore season in 1982. That year, he caught 66 passes for 1,129 yards and 7 touchdowns. In a game against Tennessee State, he set a Division I-AA college record by gaining 279 receiving yards. Coach Cooley was so impressed he told reporters that Jerry "could catch a BB in the dark."

Coach Cooley's remark inspired the Delta Devils players to give Jerry a nickname. They decided to call him "World," meaning that Jerry was so good, he could catch anything in the world.

Jerry wasn't the only one on the team with a nickname. Willie Totten, the Delta Devils' freshman quarterback, was called "Satellite" after he said he liked to beam passes to his receivers. Coach Cooley had a nickname, too. He was called "The Gunslinger" because he had his team use a "run and gun" offense, and they were known for firing the ball off quickly.

Coach Cooley had his team pass the ball as often as possible. His motto was: "The fastest way between two points is to fly." During Jerry's junior season, in 1983, footballs were flying into his hands in record numbers.

On October 1, 1983, Jerry set a Division I-AA record by catching 24 passes in a game against Southern University. His total would have been even higher, but several of his catches were disallowed because of penalties. "It didn't matter where you put the ball, Jerry would come up with it," Willie Totten says. "It was like he had glue on his hands."

Jerry went on to set Division I-AA single-season records for most catches (102) and yards (1,450). He won All-America honors. To his surprise, reporters began asking him for interviews, and *Sports Illustrated* magazine ran a story about him with the title "He's the Catch of the Year." In the story, Delta Devils receivers coach Gloster Richardson was quoted as saying, "Jerry's hands are just beautiful. He doesn't need to use his body to catch the ball. His hands are just a gift. He's developed such concentration and his pass routes are so precise. He's so spectacular, he fires everyone up."

Jerry felt uncomfortable about the fuss being made

over him. The kind of attention he liked best came from his teammates. He had been made one of the team's captains that year. The Delta Devils were happy to have him as their leader. Whenever Jerry spoke up in the locker room or on the team bus, other players would say, "World's talking! Listen up!"

The Delta Devils weren't the only people who were listening to Jerry. That year, he met a pretty student named Jackie Mitchell. Jackie attended the University of Southern Mississippi and was visiting friends at Valley when Jerry spotted her. They started to chat. Then Jerry said, "I'm going to call you tomorrow at noon."

"I thought that was the last I'd see of him," Jackie says. "The next day he called right at noon, on the dot." Jerry and Jackie started dating. They ended up getting married in September 1987.

Another important relationship Jerry developed during his junior year was with Willie Totten. Willie had joined the team the year before as the freshman quarterback. As the 1983 season went along, Jerry and Willie discovered they had a kind of "chemistry" on the football field. In sports, chemistry is the ability players have to work together in ways that make the most of their individual talents.

Jerry and Willie developed their chemistry by spending a lot of time on the field together. Along with the other receivers, they showed up an hour early for practices to work on their timing. They also worked on keeping their passing plans flexible to fit particular game situations. "We know each other's moves so well," Willie told reporters that season. "When I look for a big play, Jerry will just be there." Jerry would later have the same kind of chemistry with San Francisco 49ers quarterback Joe Montana.

Coach Cooley decided after the season that he was going to make the most of the chemistry between Jerry and Willie. To do so, he designed a special offense he called "The Satellite Express."

The Satellite Express was very different from a typical college offense. A typical college offense would run the ball more often than pass. In the Satellite Express, almost every play was a pass. Most college offenses use two running backs to run with the ball and two wide receivers to receive passes. The Satellite Express hardly ever used running backs, but featured five wide receivers.

The Delta Devils also used no huddles between plays, which is almost unheard of in college football. The huddle is a quick meeting of the players before the snap. In the huddle the players find out what play is going to be run next. At Valley, the players learned what each play was going to be by listening to Willie yell out code words or numbers before the snap. Sometimes he made hand signals. For example, if Willie put his hands to his helmet, it meant that all the receivers should go deep. Coach Cooley figured that if his team did not huddle, opposing defenses would have no time to rest. They would be left breathless from chasing the Delta Devils' speedy receivers, especially Jerry, all over the field.

Coach Cooley designed almost 200 plays for the Satellite Express. Some of these were unusual formations that had names like "Four Stack Right, Split Left." In that one, four wide receivers lined up, one right behind the other, on the right side of the field. Another wide receiver, usually Jerry, would line up by himself on the left side. At the snap, all the receivers took off down the field. Some ran long pass routes, others short. On many plays, they crisscrossed crazily back and forth to confuse defenders. Jerry usually had a precise route to run, but Coach Cooley gave him the freedom to make changes as he saw fit.

At first, Willie Totten wasn't convinced the Satellite Express would work. He quickly changed his mind after the Delta Devils soundly beat Kentucky State, 86–0, in the first game of the 1984 season. Jerry caught 17 passes for a Division I-AA record 294 yards and scored 5 touchdowns!

The Satellite Express made the Delta Devils a deadly touchdown machine. In five games, they scored 60 points or more. In the 1984 season, the Delta Devils led every team in college football in scoring with a 60.9 points-per-game average. They gained a whopping

The No-Huddle Offense

The no-huddle offense used by the Delta Devils in 1984 is not unusual today. In 1988, the Bengals made it popular in the NFL when they used it to reach the Super Bowl. The Buffalo Bills, who reached the Super Bowl in 1991, 1992, and 1993, are the best-known no-huddle team. The idea behind it is to prevent the opponent's defense from being prepared, resting, or sending in new players.

average of 637 yards per game on offense and went on to win nine games and lose only two.

Word traveled quickly about how exciting it was to watch the Delta Devils play. Attendance at their home games increased so quickly that the team had to move out of Valley's Magnolia Stadium, which held only 10,000 fans. The Devils played instead at Mississippi Memorial Stadium in nearby Jackson. There they set a stadium attendance record by drawing 63,808 fans to their game against in-state rival Alcorn State.

Jerry ran wild all season. Teams tried to cover him with three defensive backs, but it didn't matter. He again won All-America honors and set Division I-AA records with 103 receptions and 1,682 receiving yards. He was the leading scorer in Division I-AA football, with 162 points and 27 touchdown catches. He even played quarterback during a few plays and completed 6 passes for 123 yards and 5 touchdowns!

Even though Jerry had had some concerns about whether anyone in the pros would notice him playing at a small college, Jerry's great season made NFL scouts and head coaches pay attention. One of those coaches was Bill Walsh of the San Francisco 49ers. Coach Walsh got his first look at Jerry through a simple stroke of luck.

One Saturday night in October 1984, Jerry's senior season, Coach Walsh was in a hotel room in Houston, Texas. The 49ers had a game against the Oilers the next day, and he couldn't sleep. He turned on the TV in his room and started flipping through the channels. He stopped when he found college football highlights.

There on the screen was a swift, graceful receiver wearing number 88. "Nice catch," Coach Walsh thought as he watched the receiver pull in a touchdown pass. Then there was a shot of number 88 cutting away from a defender to grab another touchdown pass.

Jerry had Coach Walsh's full attention as he was shown leaving a pack of defenders in the dust while catching a third touchdown pass. Next, Coach Walsh saw the receiver running, surrounded by defenders, as he caught the ball with his hands way out in front of his body. Then he spiked the ball in the end zone. Touchdown number four!

The great plays continued. Number 88 cut across the field, caught the ball while running at full stride, and dashed into the end zone for his fifth touchdown. "The hands, the speed—what an absolutely majestic player!" Coach Walsh gasped. Then he wondered, "Hey, who is this guy?"

The answer, of course, was Jerry Rice.

Coach Walsh went to bed that night thinking about what Jerry might be able to do for the 49ers. The team already had a great offense led by Joe Montana, but it needed a wide receiver who could break games open by catching long touchdown passes. "As soon as I saw him run and catch, I knew that if we didn't get him, someday we'd be playing against him," Coach Walsh says.

The 49ers later sent scout Neil Schmidt to Mississippi Valley State to take a look at Jerry. Neil was very impressed. "I'd been a scout for 17 years," he says. "Any kind of scout at all wouldn't have to be hit by a truck to see this kid was special."

Special, indeed. By the end of the season, Jerry had set 18 Division I-AA records, including career marks for most catches (301), yards (4,693), and touchdowns (50).

Many NFL teams were still not sure Jerry was that good. Just as the college scouts had four years before, some of the NFL scouts looked at his time in the 40-yard dash and decided he was too slow. Others believed

Jerry Says Thanks

After Jerry joined the 49ers in 1985, he donated $10,000 to Mississippi Valley State University. The money was used to build a weight room for the school's athletes. Jerry also gave an autographed photo of himself to Archie Cooley. On the photo, Jerry wrote, "To Coach Cooley, I owe you everything."

he would not have set so many records if he had played against tougher competition. That wasn't really true, either. The Delta Devils played in the **Southwestern Athletic Conference**, which has a history of producing great NFL receivers.

Coach Walsh was convinced that Jerry had the talent to succeed in the NFL. "Jerry's movements were spectacular for a pass receiver, no matter what level of competition he played against," he says. "He'd been catching 100 passes year after year. We felt that if they'd throw to him that much and if he'd catch that many, he must have the basic instincts for the job."

In April 1985, shortly before he graduated from college, Jerry was drafted by the 49ers, who had beaten the Miami Dolphins in the Super Bowl that January.

Other Great NFL Receivers Who Came from the Southwestern Athletic Conference

*Harold Carmichael (Southern University): Played mostly for the Eagles from 1971 to 1984; caught 590 passes for 8,945 yards and 79 TDs; from 1972 to 1980, caught at least one pass in 127 games in a row!

*Harold Jackson (Jackson State): Played for the Rams, Eagles, Patriots, Vikings, and Seahawks from 1968 to 1983; played in five Pro Bowls; had career totals of 579 catches for 10,372 yards and 76 TDs.

*Charlie Joiner (Grambling): Played for the Oilers, Bengals, and Chargers from 1969 to 1986; played in three Pro Bowls; ranks fourth on all-time NFL reception list (750); third all-time with 12,146 yards.

*Otis Taylor (Prairie View A&M): Played for the Chiefs from 1965 to 1975; still Chiefs' all-time career leader in receiving yards (7,306) and TDs (60); played on Chiefs' Super Bowl championship team in 1970.

Jerry was the 16th player chosen in the NFL draft. Two receivers were picked ahead of him: Al Toon, by the New York Jets, and Eddie Brown, by the Cincinnati Bengals. Both went on to have fine NFL careers. Jerry went on to make history.

Getting a Grip

Most rookies, no matter how good they were in college, find life in the NFL much more difficult than they expected. Jerry certainly did.

When he arrived in **San Francisco** during the summer of 1985, Jerry was surprised to find reporters and TV cameras waiting for him. This was, after all, preseason practice. He soon saw, however, that he was now a celebrity in a big city. He had just signed a contract with the defending Super Bowl champions. The 49ers had agreed to pay him a total of more than $2.1 million during the next five years. A lot was expected of Jerry, and a lot of people would be watching him.

"Coming from Mississippi, I wasn't used to so much attention," he says. "When I first got here, I was uncomfortable. I had a hard time, but I kept myself in the right frame of mind. If not for that, I'd probably be back in Mississippi."

Jerry had to get used to living in a big city. San Francisco was full of things to do, from sightseeing to enjoying the great restaurants, nightclubs, and theaters. As a member of the 49ers, he was welcome just about everywhere. Jerry had plenty of money to go wherever he wanted and buy anything he wanted. For a while, he felt like a kid in a candy store.

Jerry drove into training camp in a flashy BMW car with license plates that said "World." He seemed cocky to his new teammates. Some of them wanted to put him in his place. They wanted to remind him that he was a rookie. They started by picking on the way he wore his hair.

Jerry's head had been shaved on the sides and there was a big pile of curls on top. Jerry's curls reminded some players of a poodle's fur, so they started calling him "Fifi." Other players called him "Bert" because they

San Francisco

San Francisco is a beautiful city on the coast of Northern California. It is famous for its cable cars, which are used to move people up and down the steep, hilly streets. About 750,000 people live there and about 3 million tourists visit each year.

thought he looked like the character on the TV show *Sesame Street.*

Jerry handled the teasing well. One day during training camp, the 49ers were gathered in a room watching game films. When the films ended, the lights came on and the movie screen went up. Sitting there was a Bert doll dressed in a football jersey with Jerry's number 80 on it. "Okay, that's a good one!" Jerry laughed.

Jerry's teammates didn't make fun of him after they saw him in action. "He's going to be a star! He's a natural," wide receiver Dwight Clark said the first time he saw Jerry catching passes in practice.

Unfortunately, Jerry's natural talent seemed to desert him as training camp went along. He began dropping passes in practice. The 49ers called Coach Cooley at Mississippi Valley State for advice on how to get Jerry back on track. Coach Cooley suggested that Jerry catch 50 extra passes before practice and 50 more after. The extra practice helped, but when the 49ers started playing exhibition games that August, Jerry's game continued to fall apart.

Jerry played miserably in his first appearance in front of the fans at Candlestick Park, the 49ers' home stadium. The 49ers were leading the Denver Broncos, 10–0, in the first quarter when Jerry dropped a pass on the Broncos' 20-yard line. In the second quarter, he ran forward before the ball was snapped, and the referee called an illegal-motion penalty. The penalty disqualified a pass completion to receiver Derrick Harmon at the Broncos' 10-yard line. In the fourth quarter, Jerry dropped another pass in Denver territory. A few minutes later, he caught a pass on the Denver 20, but the catch didn't count because he had stepped out of bounds while running to catch the ball.

Jerry's blunders were one of the reasons why the 49ers scored only three more points in the game and lost, 20–13. Reporters who covered the game wrote that Jerry might not be as good as the 49ers thought. Some stories noted that he seemed afraid after he was hit by a few hard tackles. **Coach Walsh** disagreed and later told reporters, "Jerry Rice made mental errors in this game, but he is learning and we understand that. Most rookies start slowly."

Receiver Freddie Solomon, Jerry's teammate, said, "I'm sure he was a little nervous. He's a great competitor. As time goes on, I know all of his natural talent will surface."

Jerry was still upbeat after the game. "I had a few things I should have done a little better," he said. "But I'm still learning."

Jerry had a lot to learn. His coaches had given him a big book full of hundreds of plays that he had to memorize. When the plays are memorized, all the players on offense know automatically what they are supposed to do when the quarterback calls a play. Jerry also had to

Coach Bill Walsh: "The Genius"

Bill Walsh had a long path to his three Super Bowl wins with the 49ers in the 1980s. He had coached high school and college teams and had been an assistant NFL coach for 23 years before the 49ers hired him as head coach in January 1979. The team had had a 2–14 record the year before, and only three years later, San Francisco was 16-3 and the Super Bowl champion! After his third Super Bowl win in 1989, he left coaching and later became a TV broadcaster. Three years later, he returned to coaching as head coach at Stanford University outside of San Francisco.

learn to recognize what his opponents were going to do. He did this by looking at the formation the defense lined up in before each play.

Many of the 49ers' plays were very complicated. For example, if defenders guarded Jerry closely, he might try to outrun them by going deep downfield. If the defenders stayed several feet away, he might run straight down the field about 10 yards, stop suddenly, and run back toward the quarterback. But where he ran, and when, also depended on what his teammates did. If a pass was supposed to go to another receiver, let's say Freddie Solomon, and Jerry wasn't covered closely, he might go deep instead of cutting back toward the quarterback. By going deep, he took his defender away from the part of the field where Freddie was supposed to go.

If memorizing all those plays and variations seems hard, it is. Just think of the hardest test you ever studied for in school. Multiply by 10 the amount of information you had to study. Now imagine having only a few seconds to come up with the correct answer to a question while 200-pound tacklers chase you in front of 60,000 screaming people! That's a rough idea of what Jerry had to learn in his rookie season in the NFL.

It took Jerry a long time to get a grip on everything. After the first eight games of the regular season, he had 18 receptions for 295 yards and one touchdown, but he had also dropped 10 passes and made many mistakes. Most of the mistakes happened while he was running his pass routes.

In college, Jerry had been given the freedom to run just about anywhere he wanted to go as long as he got open. With the 49ers, all the receivers were expected to go exactly where each play required them to go. There were many times when Joe Montana wanted to pass to Jerry but couldn't find him because Jerry had changed his route. Each time that happened, receivers coach Paul Hackett would be waiting for Jerry on the sideline.

Jerry's Number

When Jerry joined the 49ers in 1985, he wanted to wear number 88, as he had done in college. But that number had already been taken by receiver Freddie Solomon, who played for the 49ers from 1978 to 1985. Freddie left the team after the 1985 season, but Jerry decided to keep number 80 anyway.

"He'd say, 'Jerry, you can't do that. You're not at Mississippi Valley State anymore,'" Jerry says.

The more mistakes Jerry made and the more passes he dropped, the more frustrated and confused he became. "If I dropped a ball, I would go back to the bench and think about it too much," he says. "Then I'd drop another. I would drop one and it would cause me to drop two. I couldn't understand it. I'd never done that before and I really got down on myself. I wore gloves for a while thinking they would help, but I realized my hands weren't the problem. It was my confidence."

Many reporters and fans thought Jerry was dropping passes because he was afraid of hard tackles. Joe Montana knew that wasn't true. In the first game of the regular season, Jerry had made a leaping catch in the middle of the field. That is where there are more defenders and thus more chances of a receiver getting hit. Catching passes near the sideline is safer because there are fewer defenders and a receiver can step out of bounds to avoid a hit.

"Jerry showed that he wasn't afraid to go across the middle—the most dangerous spot for a receiver—to catch a pass," Joe wrote in his autobiography, *Audibles: My Life in Football.* "I try not to throw the ball in that spot to any receiver, but I felt great knowing that 'World' would go anywhere to catch one of my passes."

Joe thought Jerry's biggest problem was that he was trying too hard. "He was trying to make a big play every time," Joe says. "That's typical for a rookie. He tried running with the ball before he caught it. He needed to relax."

It isn't easy to relax when 60,000 fans are booing you. When Jerry dropped two passes in the first half of a home game against the Kansas City Chiefs on November 17, 1985, the crowd jeered so much that Jerry cried in the locker room at halftime. "I remember the other players comforting him," Coach Walsh says. "We won that game, but he learned the cold facts of NFL life."

The following Monday night, in a home game against the Seattle Seahawks that was shown on national TV, Jerry dropped three more passes and was booed again. "I felt like just taking off my stuff and going to the locker room," Jerry says. "I was having a terrible season. Terrible. If you don't have a level head, you can give up. But I kept fighting."

The fans were upset mostly because the 49ers were struggling. They were expected to return to the Super Bowl, but after 12 games, their record was only 7–5 and they were in second place in their division, the NFC West. The fans were disappointed that Jerry had not helped the team as much as they had expected he would.

Joe Montana was convinced that Jerry was going to be okay. "There's a difference between a guy who's catching the ball and then dropping it, and a guy who can't catch," Joe says. "You could just watch Jerry go down the field, just the way he ran, and you could see he was a player."

Still, some 49er players were starting to have doubts that Jerry was going to be able to do the job. "We told ourselves it's a matter of time before he comes around, and then we hoped we were right," says Randy Cross.

The 49ers' game against the Washington Redskins on December 1 was a turning point for Jerry. He did not catch a single pass in that game. He then realized an important thing: he should have been studying his playbook more. He had been spending too much of his free time enjoying the nightlife in San Francisco. Jerry decided to stay home evenings and study. "This is a very complex offense," he says. "When I mastered it and quit thinking about it, I quit dropping passes."

He also began staying after practice to work on breaking his bad habit of trying to run with the ball before he caught it. "Fred Solomon—he was a quarterback in college—would throw to me for 20 or 30 minutes while I concentrated on watching the ball all the way into my hands," Jerry says.

Jerry shone at last in a televised Monday night game against the Los Angeles Rams on December 9. In front of a home crowd of 61,472, he caught 10 passes for a team record 241 yards. He also scored a 66-yard touchdown and caught a 52-yard pass that set up another touchdown.

The 49ers lost, 27–20, but it was clear that Jerry had arrived. "He showed us quite a lot tonight," Coach Walsh said.

Highlights of Jerry's Rookie NFL Season: 1985

*He set a team record for rookies with 927 receiving yards.

*He set a team record with 241 receiving yards in a game against the Los Angeles Rams.

*He led all 49ers receivers with an average gain of 18.9 yards per catch.

*He was named NFC Rookie of the Year.

Jerry now believes that that Monday night game against the Rams was one of his most important. "That one game, I would say, started my career," he says. "After that, I felt I could do the job."

Jerry finished the season with 49 receptions and 4 touchdowns, 3 receiving and one rushing. His 927 receiving yards set a team record for rookies. Best of all, his struggles were rewarded when he was chosen the NFC Rookie of the Year. He also got his first taste of post-season competition.

On December 29, 1985, the 49ers met the New York Giants in a playoff game in Giants Stadium. Playing against a tough defense led by the great line-backer Lawrence Taylor, Jerry caught 4 passes for 45 yards, but the 49ers lost, 17–3.

The season ended on a down note, but Jerry had a lot to be proud of. It wasn't an easy rookie season, but he had worked through some very difficult times. He had begun to show the world what he could do. And, as it turned out, Jerry could do quite a lot.

Star on the Rise

Jerry's second season went much more smoothly. Full of confidence, he led the National Football Conference with 86 receptions and the NFL with 1,570 receiving yards. Only two receivers in NFL history had ever gained more yards in one season: Charley Hennigan of the Houston Oilers with 1,746 in 1961, and Lance Alworth of the San Diego Chargers with 1,602 in 1965.

In that 1986 season, Jerry twice tied a team record by catching three touchdown passes in a game. He finished the season with 15 scoring receptions. He earned All-Pro honors for the first time and played in his first Pro Bowl. The Pro Bowl is the NFL's all-star game. Players are chosen for it by their fellow players.

Remarkably, Jerry accomplished all those things even though his favorite quarterback, Joe Montana, missed eight games because of a back injury. Jeff Kemp and Mike Moroski, the quarterbacks who replaced Joe, were not as good, but Jerry never missed a beat.

In his first game with Jeff Kemp at quarterback, Jerry hauled in a 66-yard touchdown pass against the Los Angeles Rams. Against the Indianapolis Colts on October 5, 1986, Jerry and Jeff hooked up on touchdown passes of 58, 16, and 45 yards. Jeff was happy that Jerry was making him look so good. "If you put the ball out there anywhere near him, he'll adjust at full speed and get it," Jeff told reporters.

"He's phenomenal," 49ers running back Roger Craig said. "He can do so many things and he hasn't done it all. Last year he had trouble catching the ball because he was thinking too much. Now he thinks touchdown as soon as he catches it."

From time to time, Jerry dropped passes or made mistakes. But he got through the rough spots in the season without getting down on himself. There was a stretch of three games between October 19 and November 2 in which Jerry caught only 11 passes for 151 yards and one touchdown. But right after that, on November 9, he welcomed Joe Montana back to the starting lineup by catching 4 passes for 156 yards and 3 touchdowns against the St. Louis (now Phoenix) Cardinals.

There was no doubt that Jerry was reaching the great potential the 49ers had seen in him when he had been in college. "We had high expectations and he's certainly fulfilled all of them, or more," Coach Walsh told reporters during the season.

Jerry received a lot of praise from his opponents. "He is playing great," New York Giants head coach Bill Parcells said. "He might be the best guy in the league right now."

Giants defensive coordinator Bill Belichick added, "A lot of times, Jerry's covered, but he jumps up and gets the ball. They design plays for him and change them every week. I don't think there's a better receiver now."

Because Jerry was being paid well for what he did, he began spending his money on expensive things. It wasn't long before Jerry's coaches and teammates were joking about the expensive suits and outfits he wore. "Do you want to know what the fashion-conscious are wearing?" asked Dennis Green, the 49ers' new receivers coach. "Check out Jerry."

"He's got some clothes, I don't even know what they are," said Jerry's father. Jerry's fiancée, Jackie, said, "He spends more time in front of the mirror than I do."

He bought a Porsche for himself and a Jaguar for Jackie. He was able to fulfill the dream that he and his brother Tom had had in high school: Jerry bought his parents a new house in Starkville. He also gave them a satellite dish so that they could watch all his games on TV. He bought a condominium in Redwood City, California, near the 49ers' training camp, so that he and Jackie would have a nice place to live when they got married. "I've got to have good things around me for me to play good," Jerry says. "That's the only way I see it."

Jerry also continued to have a reputation as a nut about neatness. He ironed his jeans and always made sure the sleeves of his T-shirts were rolled up just so. Some sportswriters joked that Jerry made Felix Unger, the ridiculously neat character in the TV show *The Odd Couple*, look like a total slob. "Sometimes when he gets home and you think he'd be tired, he starts cleaning and straightening things out," Jackie says. "I tell him, 'Would you sit down!'"

With Jerry tearing up the league and **Joe Montana** healthy again, the 49ers rolled to a 10–5–1 record. They finished first in the NFC West and took on the Giants again in the playoffs. Many people remember

Joe Montana

Many people think Joe Montana is the greatest NFL quarterback of all time. He led the University of Notre Dame to a national college championship in 1977. He was then drafted by the 49ers in 1979. Since then, he has won two NFL MVP awards, been selected for six Pro Bowls, and led the 49ers to four Super Bowl wins. Joe's three Super Bowl MVP awards are a record.

the game because of Jerry. Unfortunately, it was for a reason Jerry would like to forget.

The first time the 49ers had the ball, they began driving down the field. They were around the 50-yard line when Joe Montana threw a pass right to Jerry as Jerry was running across the middle of the field. Jerry burst away from the Giants' defenders and had a clear path to the end zone. Joe was so sure Jerry was going to score that he raised his arms to signal a touchdown. Suddenly, the ball just popped out of Jerry's hands. It rolled into the end zone, where it was recovered by the Giants. New York promptly marched back down the field for a touchdown and went on to win, 49–3!

The loss wasn't Jerry's fault. The Giants were a very good team. They won the Super Bowl three weeks later.

Highlights of Jerry's Second NFL Season: 1986

*He led the NFL with 1,570 receiving yards and 15 touchdown catches.

*He set a team record for most touchdown catches in a season (15).

*He was named All-Pro.

*He was named NFL Player of the Year by Sports Illustrated.

But some people felt that the fumble made the 49ers lose their confidence and that they might have played better if Jerry had scored.

Fans and sportswriters debated about Jerry's goof for days after the game. Jerry was embarrassed and a bit angry with himself. "I have to clean that up," he said.

The day after the game, Jerry began working out. He was determined to have his best season ever—and he did.

Flash 80

On June 7, 1987, Jerry and Jackie celebrated the birth of their first child, a daughter they named Jaqui. Jerry liked his role as a new father. "I'll be lying there asleep and Jerry will hear the baby before I do," Jackie told reporters. "He's the one to get up and take care of her and he has to be at work at eight o'clock in the morning."

In training camp that summer, Jerry's teammates could see that he was all set to have a big season. "Jerry's looking like Jerry," Ronnie Lott said one day after practice. "The workhorse with the great work ethic."

In early August, Jerry saw where that work ethic could lead him. The 49ers traveled to Canton, Ohio, the home of the Pro Football Hall of Fame, to play the Kansas City Chiefs in the Hall of Fame Game. "When we were there, I went in the Hall," Jerry says. "It sent chills through me. That's where I want to go."

The following week, Jerry broke his finger in practice and missed the 49ers' exhibition game against the Cowboys. As Jerry sat in the stands and watched the game, his body twitched and jerked as if he were on the field running pass patterns against the Dallas defensive backs. "My wife thinks I'm crazy," Jerry told reporters. Jackie added that Jerry often twitched and moved like that in his sleep!

There was no question that Jerry was ready to start the season once his finger healed. The 49ers opened the regular season by beating the Pittsburgh Steelers, 30–17, with Jerry catching eight passes for 106 yards and a touchdown. "Covering Jerry is a horror show," Steelers defensive back Dwayne Woodruff said. "He's so smooth when he's running. He gets right on top of you and before you know it, he's by you. Once he is, I don't think anybody's going to catch him."

Very few defensive backs did catch him that season. Jerry caught 65 passes for 1,078 yards and set an NFL record with 22 touchdown receptions. The most amazing thing was that he set the record even though the NFL players went on strike for four games. (The players wanted the right to become "free agents" who could play for any team they wished once their contracts with their original teams expired. The team owners refused and used substitute players until the NFL players' union gave up and ended the strike.)

The old NFL record of 18 touchdown catches in one season was set in 1984 by Mark Clayton of the

Pro Football Hall of Fame Receiver–Quarterback Duos

Jerry Rice and QB Joe Montana will one day be elected to the Pro Football Hall of Fame. Here are some pairs already in the Hall:

*With QB John Unitas, Raymond Berry led the Baltimore Colts to NFL championships in 1958 and 1959.

*Don Maynard and QB Joe Namath are best remembered for leading the New York Jets to victory over the Colts in the 1969 Super Bowl.

*Washington Redskins Charley Taylor and QB Sonny Jurgensen were always among the NFL's receiving and passing leaders from 1964 to 1974. Charley played in eight Pro Bowls.

Miami Dolphins in 15 games. Jerry needed only 11 games to break that mark. He also set another NFL record by catching at least one touchdown pass 13 games in a row.

"For a receiver to be that consistent is remarkable," says Hall of Fame wide receiver Lynn Swann, who played for the Steelers from 1974 to 1982. "Anybody can make a big catch for a touchdown, but to do it game after game is remarkable."

Jerry's record-breaking season was due largely to the chemistry he had developed with Joe Montana. It was the same kind of chemistry he had shared with Willie Totten in college. It was the result of many, many hours of practicing, playing, and talking about football together.

"I've been playing with Joe for three years now and we know each other," Jerry explained to reporters. "I know exactly where he's going to put the ball. My job is just to get to that spot. We really make a lot of things work that are totally crazy. We look at it on film and it seems like we just invent our own plays at times."

Those times were usually when Joe called an "audible" before the snap. Audibles are spoken signals that a quarterback uses to tell his teammates that the play he called in the huddle has been changed. Joe used audibles whenever he could see that his offense wouldn't work against the opposing team's defense. He would then change the play to one he thought would catch that particular defense by surprise.

Here's an example: Let's say the 49ers are playing the Rams. In the huddle, Joe calls a handoff to running back Roger Craig. When the 49ers line up, Joe looks at the way the Rams' defense is lined up. He sees that some of the defensive backs are standing close to the line of scrimmage. That usually means they are going to rush the quarterback, which is called a blitz. Joe reasons that if he hands off the ball, there's a good chance Roger will be tackled right away by a blitzing defensive back. So Joe calls an audible that tells his teammates the play is changing to a quick, short pass to Jerry. Joe knows that if the defensive backs blitz, the Rams will have fewer players staying back to cover Jerry and the other 49er receivers.

Jerry, too, had become very good at "reading" defensive formations. Sometimes it seemed he could read Joe's mind as well. "I know exactly what defenses are trying to do to me," Jerry said. "Once Joe starts to audible, I just smile because I know there will be one-on-one coverage and I'll be open."

Covering Jerry with one defensive back was almost impossible, as some teams learned the hard way that season. On September 20, 1987, the 49ers were trailing the Bengals, 26–20, with two seconds left in the game. They had the ball on Cincinnati's 25-yard line. Jerry lined up against defensive back Eric Thomas. Jerry took off for the end zone and left Eric behind with a leaping catch for a touchdown. The 49ers won, 27–26.

On November 22, Jerry got three touchdown catches, despite being covered by Rod Jones of the Tampa Bay Buccaneers. "One man should not be that good," Rod said after the game.

Jerry had become a master at fooling defenders. As he runs his pass routes, Jerry moves his head or hips in ways that make the defender think he is going to cut one way when he is really going somewhere else. "What makes Jerry so special is his body language," says Steve Young, who was the 49ers' backup quarterback that season. "I've never seen anything like it, what he can do to a defensive back. Yet at the same time, the quarterback can read him perfectly. I know where he's going to go."

Jerry also fooled defensive backs with his speed. It was well known around the league that he was not a very fast runner, so defenders were often surprised by his quickness and the way he used his speed.

"It's the speed of my first five steps," Jerry says. "My first five steps are *right now*. I'm on you. I accelerate into my cuts and accelerate again coming out of them. I amaze myself sometimes. I don't really know where the extra speed comes from."

Washington Redskins defensive back Barry Wilburn said, "He's probably not considered a speed demon. But I'll tell you what: when the ball is up, he goes and gets it as well as anyone in the league. That's great speed as far as I'm concerned."

Jerry's teammates thought he was pretty speedy, too. They gave him a new nickname: "Flash." During games that season, Jerry started wearing a small white towel with "Flash 80" written on it. ("Flash" was the nickname; "80" was his uniform number.) He tucked one end of the towel into the waistband of his uniform pants so that it fluttered from his hip as he ran.

Some defensive backs resented Jerry's towel. They thought he was a showoff for wearing it. "I wasn't trying to show them up," Jerry says. "The towel was my inspiration. Before every game I would sit in front of my locker and draw the design onto the towel as I concentrated on the game plan. I did it because the idea motivated me."

After five games, NFL officials ordered Jerry to stop wearing the towel. The league had a rule against players' wearing anything but their official uniforms during games. Jerry wrote "Flash 80" on the bottom of his cleats and went right on driving his opponents crazy.

Before the 49ers played the Cleveland Browns on November 29, Browns defensive back Hanford Dixon vowed, "We're going to stay in Rice's face all day." Jerry made Hanford look foolish by catching 7 passes for 126 yards and 3 touchdowns as the 49ers won, 38–24. One of his receptions was an amazing one near the sideline in which he leaped, stretched out, caught the ball over his shoulder, and somehow landed with his knees in bounds. "It looked like he stopped in mid-air to catch the ball," 49ers receivers coach Dennis Green said.

On December 6 against the Green Bay Packers, Jerry made what he called his best catch of the season. It was a 57-yard touchdown play in the fourth quarter. He was running at full speed diagonally across the field. Two defensive backs were covering him. Joe Montana had to throw the pass low to keep it out of reach of the defenders. Jerry reached down and grabbed the far side of the ball as it went by. Then he exploded past two more tacklers and into the end zone.

All season long, Jerry was in a zone of his own. "It's unreal," he told reporters. "Once the ball's thrown to me, I don't hear anything. No footsteps, no crowd. And I don't see anything except the ball."

Jerry's biggest day was against the Atlanta Falcons on December 20 at San Francisco's Candlestick Park. Early in the second half, he caught a 20-yard touchdown pass that broke Mark Clayton's record for the most scoring receptions in a season. The catch also broke the record for most games in a row (11) with at least one touchdown reception. That record had been set by Hall of Famer Elroy "Crazylegs" Hirsch of the Rams in 1950–51 and tied by Buddy Dial of the Steelers in 1959–60.

Jerry ended his record-breaking day with two scoring catches, plus a touchdown he scored on a running play in the 49ers' 35–7 victory. "I think it's fantastic," 49ers center Randy Cross told reporters after the game. "But we'd get more excited if he was more excited. He has so much talent and just seems to take things in stride. We want to jump up and down with him, but he just says, 'Thank you.'"

"The most important thing to me is we won," Jerry said.

The following week, the 49ers ended the regular

Jerry has caught more touchdown passes than anyone else in National Football League history. Many
people believe he is the best receiver in the game.

Jerry's dad, Joe, was a bricklayer who built this house for his wife, Eddie B., and their family. Jerry developed strong hands like his dad's (shown) by working with him during summers as a teenager.

Jerry finished his four years at Mississippi Valley State in 1984 with 18 Division I-AA records, including college career marks for most catches (301), yards (4,693), and touchdowns (50).

In college, Jerry liked working with his hands off the football field, too. That's why he studied auto mechanics, and health and physical education.

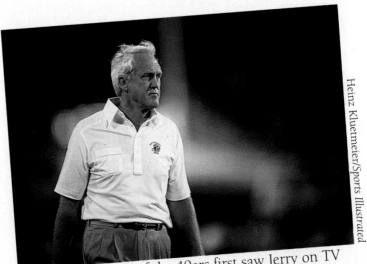

Coach Bill Walsh of the 49ers first saw Jerry on TV scoring five touchdowns in one college football game. He knew then he wanted Jerry on his team!

Jerry learned to change direction quickly by chasing horses when he was a kid. Now he uses that skill to avoid being tackled.

Jerry has taken a lot of kidding about some of his hairstyles. This one had his teammates calling him "Fifi" because it reminded them of the way a poodle's fur is trimmed.

AT **B.L. MOOR HIGH SCHOOL JERRY** WAS ON THE TRACK AND BASKETBALL TEAMS. HE DIDN'T THINK MUCH ABOUT FOOTBALL UNTIL HE CUT CLASS ONE DAY AND GOT CAUGHT BY THE VICE-PRINCIPAL...

JERRY MADE THE TEAM AND HE WORKED HARD TO IMPROVE HIS SKILLS...

In Super Bowl XXIII—played in January 1989—Jerry (number 80) caught a total of 11 passes for 215 yards, a Super Bowl record. He was named Most Valuable Player.

Jerry and the 49ers won the 1990 Super Bowl by the amazing score of 55–10. This was just one of three touchdown receptions Jerry made in that game, a Super Bowl record.

After the 49ers won their second Super Bowl in a row, Jerry held the winners' Vince Lombardi Trophy. It is named in honor of the famous former coach of the Green Bay Packers.

Jerry (left) and quarterback Joe Montana (center) were a great team. They set several NFL records in the 1989 and 1990 Super Bowls thanks to their good chemistry.

Jerry was joined by his wife, Jackie, and their daughter, Jaqui, for the parade which celebrated the 49ers' win in the 1990 Super Bowl. Since then, they've had a son, Jerry Jr.

season with a 13–2 record by shutting out the Rams, 48–0. Jerry caught two more touchdown passes and became the first wide receiver to lead the league in scoring since "Crazylegs" Hirsch had in 1951.

Jerry won a lot of awards: National Football Conference Most Valuable Player from his fellow players; the Bert Bell Award as pro player of the year from the Maxwell Football Club; the NFL Player of the Year Award from the Touchdown Club of Washington, D.C.; the Len Eshmont Award for inspirational and courageous play from the 49ers; the Jim Thorpe Memorial Trophy from the Newspaper Enterprise Association; the NFL Most Valuable Player Award from the Pro Football Writers Association; the Offensive Player of the Year Award from the Associated Press; and NFL Player of the Year awards from *Sports Illustrated*, *Pro Football Weekly*, *The Sporting News*, and *Football Digest*. And, of course, he was named All-Pro and chosen to start in the Pro Bowl.

Having such a great season meant Jerry got a lot of attention from the media. The attention still made him feel uncomfortable, and he was concerned about his image. He spoke with a thick southern accent and didn't always use correct grammar. He hired Sylvester Jackson, a radio personality in the San Francisco Bay area, to help him with public speaking. "If you're going to be a public figure and a role model to kids, you may as well do everything the right way," Jerry says.

Jerry had done everything the right way on the field. "I don't think there's ever been a receiver that had the type of year he's had," Steelers defensive back Dwayne Woodruff said. "It's one thing to catch a touchdown pass when the defense is off guard. It's another thing to do it when everybody in the world knows you're going to get the ball."

"He's scary," Joe Montana said. "If Jerry isn't the best receiver in football, he's pretty darn close to it. He's just a great athlete."

In the playoffs, the 49ers met the Vikings. The game was expected to be an exciting contest between Jerry and Anthony Carter, the Vikings' fine young wide

Highlights of Jerry's Third NFL Season: 1987

*He was named the NFL's Most Valuable Player.

*He set an NFL record with 22 touchdown catches.

*He set an NFL record by catching touchdown passes 13 games in a row.

*He led the NFL in scoring with 138 points, the most ever scored in one season by a wide receiver.

*He was named All-Pro and played in the Pro Bowl.

receiver. Unfortunately, Jerry strained the hamstring in his right leg in practice, and two days before the game, it felt so sore he couldn't even bend over and touch his toes.

The crowd in Candlestick Park was stunned when the Vikings scored three touchdowns the first three times they had the ball, and then scored a fourth touchdown on an interception. Joe and Jerry struggled all afternoon. Joe was scrambling constantly and completed only 5 of 12 passes for 58 yards before he was taken out of the game. Jerry made only 3 catches for a measly 28 yards. Anthony Carter caught 10 passes for a playoff game record of 227 yards as the Vikings won, 36–24.

For Jerry, the loss was a sour end to a glorious season filled with records and awards. "The only thing I have to hang on to is the awards," he said after the game. "The season didn't end like I wanted. It's disappointing that I didn't play better."

Coach Walsh was asked by reporters if he expected Jerry to be even better next season. "Sure he will be better," he replied. "It may be that his statistics won't improve, but, yes, he will be better."

Coach Walsh was right, thanks to Jerry's hard work all winter and spring to make it happen.

Ghostbuster

After only three seasons in the NFL, Jerry had earned a reputation as the best wide receiver in the league. In June 1988, the 49ers rewarded him with a new contract that would pay him a little more than $5 million over the next five seasons.

Jerry seemed to have it all. Yet there was still something he wanted very much: to play in the Super Bowl.

During most of the 1988 season, it looked as if Jerry would have to wait at least another year to get his wish. After 11 games, the 49ers had a 6–5 record. Even their most die-hard fans were worried that they might not make the playoffs.

What was wrong with the team? One thing was that there was a lot of uncertainty about which quarterback, Joe Montana or Steve Young, would be starting each game. There was also a question about whether the starting quarterback would finish the game. Coach Walsh was experimenting with his lineup. It didn't help that Joe Montana kept getting hurt. During the course of the season, he bruised his elbow, injured his ribs, and hurt his back. He missed all or parts of five games. His injuries caused him to struggle when he did play.

The offensive line struggled, too, and made mistakes at crucial moments in games. "We didn't know what was going on," San Francisco guard Guy McIntyre says. "All of a sudden, everything was going wrong. We were getting all these penalties called against us. One day Coach Walsh really screamed at us. He said we weren't getting the job done. We didn't know what was happening."

There were also games in which the defense collapsed. The 49ers were beaten, 34–17, by the Atlanta Falcons on September 18. On November 6, they blew a 23–0 lead against the Phoenix Cardinals and lost, 24–23.

Jerry had his share of problems, too. His streak of scoring a touchdown in every game ended at 13 with the first game of the season, against New Orleans. In the second game of the season, on September 11, he dropped three passes. He then came back to help beat the New York Giants with a 78-yard touchdown catch with 42 seconds left in the game. Two weeks later, he had three touchdown receptions against the Seattle Seahawks. After that, however, he caught only one touchdown pass and failed to gain more than 86 receiving yards in any of his next seven games.

Opponents were working harder than ever to stop

Jerry. They learned ways to disguise what they were going to do so that Jerry couldn't read their defensive formations before the snap. For example, the defensive backs might line up as though they were going to cover Jerry one-on-one. Then he would find three backs covering him as soon as he started to run.

Jerry grew frustrated as the season went on and the 49ers kept struggling. "I feel I can contribute to the team a little more [than I am]," Jerry told reporters. "I don't think I'm as sharp as I was last year."

Jerry then injured his right ankle in a game against the Los Angeles Rams on October 16. The ankle bothered him for most of the rest of the season. He couldn't run as well or cut as sharply as he had before, and defenders took advantage of this. Against the Minnesota Vikings on October 30, Jerry caught only one pass for 22 yards. Jerry didn't like talking about how things were going, so he started avoiding reporters.

The 49ers pulled themselves together in the nick of time. After losing 9–3 to the Los Angeles Raiders on November 13, the players held a meeting. They discussed the team's problems and decided to try harder. Then they went out and beat the Washington Redskins, 37-21, the following week.

Jerry got himself back on track against the Redskins by catching 3 passes for 105 yards and a touchdown. Then he topped that performance with 6 catches for 171 yards and 2 touchdowns against the San Diego

Chargers on November 27. In that game, he also set a team record for longest touchdown reception by scoring on a 96-yard play.

The 49ers ended up winning four of their last five games, and they qualified for the playoffs. Jerry was determined to do well in the post-season. He wanted to make up for a disappointing regular season in which he caught 64 passes for 1,306 yards and 9 touchdowns, 13 fewer than he scored in 1987.

"I thought I would come back and have an even better season than last year," Jerry told reporters. "It didn't work out, but I've still got a shot at the Super Bowl. If we win the Super Bowl, it will have been a great year. Otherwise it was a disappointing year for me with the injury. I feel like I didn't play like the real Jerry Rice."

Jerry also wanted to silence the criticism he was hearing about his past failures in post-season play. Some sportswriters were wondering why he never seemed to be much of a factor in big games.

Jerry had a lot of playoff ghosts haunting him. There were the 4 catches for only 45 yards against the Giants in 1985, the surprising fumble against the Giants in 1986, the three catches for just 28 yards against the Minnesota Vikings in 1987, and the unbelievable fact that Jerry had yet to score a touchdown in a playoff game.

Jerry started busting those ghosts when the 49ers

met the Vikings on New Year's Day 1989. He caught 5 passes for 61 yards and tied a playoff game record with 3 touchdown receptions. After his first score, Jerry was so happy he hugged a cameraman standing near the end zone. Jerry patted the man on the head and said, "Happy New Year!"

All three of Jerry's touchdowns came in the first half, and they caught Minnesota's defense completely off guard. The Vikings had been expecting Jerry to go deep for long passes. Instead, he surprised them by scoring on short plays of 2, 4, and 11 yards.

"It's frustrating because you don't expect that of Jerry Rice," Vikings defensive back Carl Lee said after the 49ers had won the game, 34–9. "If you keep him from beating you deep, you feel like you've done your job. Then that happens."

Next up for Jerry and the 49ers were the Chicago Bears. The game was played at Soldier Field in Chicago, where the temperature was a bone-chilling 17 degrees at game time. Howling 29-mile-per-hour winds made the air feel as if it was 26 degrees below zero!

Some experts thought the 49ers might lose because they were used to playing most of their games in the warm California climate. Jerry wasn't worried, though. "I'll catch the ball in any kind of weather," he told reporters the day before the game. "I'm going to have a big game tomorrow."

During the pre-game warmups, Joe Montana saw

Steve Young throwing passes that fluttered wildly in the wind. Joe walked over to Jerry. "This wind makes it tough to throw accurately downfield," Joe said. "We'll have to play some basketball. I'll probably be throwing the ball high and you'll have to go up and get it."

That's just what Jerry did. In the first quarter, the 49ers had the ball on their own 39-yard line when Joe threw a high pass about 20 yards. Jerry jumped up, came down with the ball, and cut around Bears defensive back Mike Richardson. Another defensive back, Todd Krumm, ran at him. Jerry stopped suddenly and took a step backward, like a bullfighter dodging a bull. Todd flew by, missing the tackle, and Jerry took off for a 61-yard touchdown.

In the second quarter, Joe hit Jerry with a 27-yard touchdown pass. The 49ers went on to an easy 28–3 win that sent them to the Super Bowl in Miami, Florida, where they would play the Cincinnati Bengals.

Jerry was thrilled. Here, at last, was his chance to show the world what he could do in the biggest football game of all. Nothing was going to stop him, not even an injury.

When Jerry hurt his right ankle in practice six days before the game, a grim Coach Walsh told reporters, "Jerry Rice will be questionable to play this game."

"Can the 49ers win without him?" a reporter asked.

"Our offense really needs Rice to perform the way it

can," Coach Walsh replied. "To be without him would make this game very difficult. He is the big-play man in our offense. The last six weeks he has been playing at his peak."

Jerry wasn't worried. "My teammates know I'm going to fight my way back and I'm not going to give up," he said.

Jerry missed two days of practice. Then he was spotted dancing at a nightclub in Miami. When the Bengals heard about it, some of them thought Jerry was faking his injury. "I think it might be a trick," defensive back Eric Thomas said. "Jerry Rice is going to be ready for this game."

That was true, but not because Jerry was faking his injury. Jerry had to take it easy in his final practices before the big game. Meanwhile, the Bengal defensive backs boasted that they were going to turn Jerry into Rice pudding. They wore T-shirts that said "SWAT Team" ("SWAT" is a police term that stands for Special Weapons and Tactics) and told reporters they were going to hit Jerry hard every chance they got.

"He's only human, you know," defensive back Lewis Billups said. "He won't be able to handle [getting hit hard]."

"I want the guy bad," Eric Thomas said. "I want the guy real bad."

Jerry wasn't fazed by all the boasting. "I'm not going

to get into it with Eric Thomas," he said. "I'm not the kind of player who talks. I just go out and perform. Eric's got to show up on Sunday and so do I. We'll take it from there."

When game day finally arrived, Jerry was ready to go. Tears welled up in his eyes as he stood on the sideline and listened to the national anthem before the opening kickoff. Watching from the stands at Joe Robbie Stadium was a sellout crowd of 75,129 people, including Jerry's wife, daughter, parents, brothers, and

Highlights of Jerry's Fourth NFL Season: 1988

*He led the team with 1,306 receiving yards.

*He set a team record with a 96-yard touchdown against the Chargers on November 27.

*He tied an NFL record by scoring six touchdowns in post-season play.

*He set a Super Bowl record with 215 receiving yards against the Bengals.

*He was named All-Pro and selected for the Pro Bowl.

*He was named MVP of the Super Bowl.

sisters. "This was my dream come true," he says.

It turned out to be a very sweet dream. The 49ers' offense struggled most of the game against the tough Bengals defense. But when the going really got tough, whom did they call? The Ghostbuster. Time and time again, Jerry came through when his team needed him most, chasing away those haunting images of playoffs past. Nine of his 11 catches in the game gave the 49ers first downs. His touchdown catch in the fourth quarter tied the game at 13–13. To complete the game-winning touchdown drive in the final three minutes, the 49ers gained 92 yards, 51 of them on three passes to Jerry. He did not score the winning touchdown, but his presence on the field made Bengals defensive back Ray Horton freeze just long enough for John Taylor to get open and make the big catch.

Jerry's catches were often breathtaking. He leaped and dived and made the boastful Bengal defensive backs eat their words. He beat Eric Thomas for a 31-yard gain in the third quarter and did the same to Lewis Billups for a 44-yarder in the fourth.

In all, Jerry's 215 receiving yards set a Super Bowl record. He was named the game's Most Valuable Player. Only two wide receivers—Lynn Swann of the Steelers in 1976 and Fred Biletnikoff of the Raiders in 1977—had ever won that honor.

In the locker room after the game, Jerry cried tears of joy. When he finally got himself together, he went before the TV cameras to accept the MVP trophy. The moment was made even more special when he was joined by his mom, dad, Jackie, and their daughter.

"A day I'll never forget," Jerry said. "Everyone was saying 'Jerry can't perform in the playoffs.' I had to prove to myself that I could get the job done."

Oddly enough, Jerry's dad was asked if he thought Jerry would ever spend time working with bricks again. "No, I don't think he'll be coming back to bricklaying," Mr. Rice replied. "I think he's doing what God intended him to do."

After a team party, Jerry went back to his hotel room to help Jackie pack for their trip to Hawaii. Once again, Jerry had been selected to play in the Pro Bowl, which is held each year in Honolulu. He was still so excited after his big day that he couldn't sleep.

"I stayed up all night," he says. "I felt really good. I felt like I had achieved a lot. My goal was to participate in the Super Bowl, and just to win it meant a lot to me."

Jerry had traveled a long, bumpy road to reach his goal. He had battled through injury and people's doubts about how good he could be in important games. Now they knew.

8
The Winds of Change

The joy Jerry felt after his great performance in the Super Bowl quickly changed to disappointment. People seemed to talk more about how brilliantly Joe Montana had played while leading the 49ers on their game-winning drive than about Jerry. Then, four days after the game, Coach Walsh announced that he was retiring as a coach to work as an executive for the team. (He soon left the team completely and took a job as a football broadcaster for NBC-TV.) Coach Walsh's announcement was a huge story. Suddenly, Jerry felt ignored.

One thing Jerry had expected was for companies to ask him to endorse their products, for which he would be paid, but only a few did. "I don't know if I'll get any recognition in commercials or anything," Jerry said during an interview on a radio station in San Francisco that winter. "I thought I deserved more coverage, but between Bill Walsh retiring and stories about Joe Montana, I got lost in the shuffle. I'm a real modest guy, but I went out and played my best that day. It's not that I wanted all the attention. I just wanted respect for what I achieved."

Jerry was criticized widely by the media after he said that. John C. Dvorak, a sports columnist for _The San Francisco Examiner_ newspaper, listed every picture of and every story about Jerry that had appeared in the local papers after the game. There were hundreds. "Folks, if this is an example of being snubbed by the media, then we should all be so lucky!" Dvorak wrote.

Sports Illustrated ran an essay by writer Ron Fimrite of San Francisco, who said that Jerry was just another athlete who cares more about endorsements than winning championships.

Everywhere Jerry went that winter, reporters asked him about his comments. He tried to explain that what he really wanted was respect for what he had done in the Super Bowl, not a lot of endorsements. Jerry got so sick of trying to defend himself that he once swore at a reporter.

When training camp opened in July 1989, Jerry was in a better mood. His attitude had changed. "I'm a totally different guy now," he told reporters. "I guess you could say I'm more mature. I think some of the things I said about not getting enough recognition were blown out of proportion. I'm not going to say I'm sorry

I said it, but I did learn from the experience. My past is behind me. The idea in sports is to keep getting better."

As usual, Jerry had not stopped trying to improve. During the off-season, he used a new daily workout routine that included lots of short sprints. The workouts helped him lose 12 pounds, made him quicker, and gave him more stamina.

Jerry's good mood didn't last very long. When the season began, he discovered that he was no longer the "big-play man" in the 49ers' offense. **George Seifert**, the team's new head coach, wanted several players to share that role.

Coach Seifert thought San Francisco's offense had become predictable. Other teams had learned that the key to beating the 49ers was stopping Jerry, Joe Montana, and running back Roger Craig. So Coach Seifert and Mike Holmgren, the new offensive coordinator, designed plays and game plans that made more use of running back Tom Rathman, tight end Brent Jones, and wide receiver John Taylor. The idea was to make other teams try to stop six key players instead of three.

The idea worked beautifully. On September 24, the 49ers trailed the Philadelphia Eagles, 21–10, in the fourth quarter. They rallied to win, 38–28, when Joe threw touchdown passes to John, Tom, Brent, and Jerry.

The 49ers had the best offense in the NFL that season. Joe Montana was the league's top quarterback.

George Seifert

George Seifert was a 49ers defensive coach for nine years before he became the team's head coach in 1989. That season, he became only the second man ever to lead his team to a Super Bowl win in his first season as a head coach. The 49ers' record of 56–13 from 1989 to 1992 earned Coach Seifert the reputation as one of the NFL's best head coaches.

Roger Craig rushed for 1,054 yards. John Taylor had a fine season with 1,077 receiving yards and 10 touchdowns. John even set a team record with 286 yards receiving against the Rams on December 11. He also scored touchdowns on plays of 92 and 95 yards in that game.

Jerry ended up having a terrific season, too. He led the NFL in receiving yards with 1,483 and led all wide receivers with 17 touchdown catches. He was named All-Pro and was selected to play in the Pro Bowl once again.

So why had Jerry been unhappy at first with the idea of change? It had a lot to do with his competitive nature as a player. Jerry wants to be the best at what he does. He takes great pride in his ability to come through in the clutch. He was upset when he realized he would not be called on as often when the 49ers needed a big play. Some of his teammates told reporters they had heard Jerry and Coach Holmgren arguing loudly about what Jerry's role would be.

"As a competitor, you want the football," Jerry told reporters when they asked him about the argument. "I'm not a selfish ballplayer, but I want the opportunity to prove to myself that I can make the plays."

As it turned out, he got many opportunities because the 49ers passed the ball often that season. Jerry ended up leading the team with 82 receptions. Tom Rathman had 73. John Taylor had 60. Roger Craig had 49, and Brent Jones had 40.

Those players caught so many passes because Coaches Seifert and Holmgren made another wise change in the 49ers' offense. They knew that the team had to have more key players. But then, early in the season, they decided it was also too difficult to complete a lot of long passes downfield to Jerry or John. Too many teams expected them. One team, the Rams, guarded against the passes by using six defensive backs instead of the usual four or five in their game with the 49ers on October 1. The Rams won, 13–12, and Jerry was held to only 2 catches for 36 yards. John Taylor didn't do any better. He caught only 3 passes for 33 yards.

After that, Coaches Seifert and Holmgren made the

49ers use more short, quick passes. Joe Montana was told to take only three steps back after the snap instead of his usual seven before he threw the ball. By taking only three steps, he was able to get rid of the ball more quickly. He could pass to a running back or receiver before the defense had time to react fully to the play. The running backs and receivers did not have time to run very far downfield before the pass was thrown, but that didn't really matter. Jerry, John, and Roger were excellent runners who could avoid tacklers and gain yards after they caught the ball.

Eight of Jerry's 17 touchdown catches that season were on plays of 11 yards or less. But the change to short passes also made great use of the quickness and stamina Jerry had gained from his sprint workouts during the off-season. He was an ace at catching short passes and taking off on long runs.

"Catch one for 5 yards and run 80," Jerry explained to reporters. "You see a lot of guys who catch the ball and then they just fall to the ground, but when I catch the ball, the fun is just starting."

Indeed it was. The 49ers finished the season with a 14–2 record and rolled into the playoffs against the Minnesota Vikings. The game showed just how difficult it was to stop the 49ers' new passing attack.

Minnesota had the best defense in the NFL that season, but Jerry and his teammates ended up having a field day against it. There were about five minutes left

The Team of the 1980's

The 49ers were the dominant team in the NFL during the 1980's. They had the best record (104–47–1); they finished first in their division seven times, appeared in the playoffs eight times, and won four Super Bowls. Jerry played in two of those Super Bowls.

in the first quarter and the 49ers were trailing, 3–0, when Jerry caught a 7-yard pass. He darted through a crowd of tacklers and ran 65 yards for a touchdown. In the second quarter, Brent Jones and John Taylor each caught 8-yard touchdown passes. Jerry followed with a 13-yard score and the 49ers led, 27–3, at halftime.

The 49ers' lightning-quick passes had the Vikings reeling. One reporter wrote that a 12-yard pass Jerry caught in the second quarter happened so fast, the ball looked like a tightly strung wire stretching from Joe Montana to Jerry. "One second, one and a half at most," TV broadcaster Terry Bradshaw said. "No way in the world you can stop that pass."

"The way they played today, no one can touch them," said Vikings center Kirk Lowdermilk after the 41–13 loss. "They'll walk into the Super Bowl."

That's what happened. The 49ers beat the Rams,

30–3, in the NFC championship game the following week. The Rams made a big mistake by expecting and guarding against long passes. The 49ers beat them with short passes and running plays. Jerry caught 6 passes for 55 yards, but the 49ers' touchdowns were scored by Brent Jones, Roger Craig, and John Taylor. Mike Cofer also kicked 3 field goals.

For the second year in a row, the 49ers went to the Super Bowl. Their opponents this time were the Denver Broncos. The game was played in the Superdome in New Orleans, Louisiana, on January 28, 1990.

The Broncos were expected to lose, but they weren't afraid of the 49ers. Denver's defensive backs were a cocky group who liked to play hard and tackle harder. During the week before the game, they promised that Jerry and John were in for a rough time. "We're going to beat Rice and Taylor up a bit," Broncos safety Dennis Smith told reporters. "They really haven't been hit a lot in the playoffs. But when they catch a ball against us, they're going to remember it."

Jerry remembered it, but not for the reason Dennis said. The first time the 49ers had the ball, they marched to the Denver 20-yard line. Then Joe Montana fired a pass to Jerry at the 8-yard line. Broncos free safety Steve Atwater tried to deliver a crunching tackle, but he just bounced off Jerry, who ran happily into the end zone for a touchdown. The rout was on.

The 49ers won, 55–10. It was the most lopsided

score in Super Bowl history. Jerry caught 7 passes for 148 yards and set a Super Bowl record with 3 touchdown receptions. All day long, he made the Denver defensive backs wish they had never opened their mouths.

"If you remember in the Super Bowl last year,"

Great Super Bowl Games by Receivers

Jerry's two record-breaking performances in the Super Bowl are among the best in the game's history. Here are some others:

*Max McGee, Green Bay, 1967: Seven receptions for 138 yards and 2 touchdowns as the Packers beat the Chiefs, 35–10.

*Lynn Swann, Pittsburgh, 1976: Named MVP after 4 catches for 161 yards and one touchdown as the Steelers beat the Cowboys, 21–17.

*Fred Biletnikoff, Oakland, 1977: Named MVP after 4 catches for 79 yards that helped set up 2 touchdowns for the Raiders' 32–14 win.

*Rickey Sanders, Washington, 1988: Nine catches for 193 yards and 2 touchdowns as the Redskins beat the Broncos, 42–10.

Highlights of Jerry's Fifth NFL Season: 1989

*He led the NFL with 1,483 receiving yards.

*He led all wide receivers with 17 touchdown catches.

*He became the 49ers' all-time leader in touchdown catches.

*He set a Super Bowl record by catching three touchdown passes against the Bengals.

*He was named All-Pro and played in the Pro Bowl.

49ers center Jesse Sapolu told reporters after the game, "Cincinnati's Lewis Billups did a lot of talking about their defensive backs stopping Jerry cold. Now, those Denver players did a lot of talking this week. I think everybody should learn one thing today: don't say anything about Jerry Rice in a Super Bowl before you play him."

Jerry said, "One thing about our receivers today was we made up our minds we were not going down on the first hit. No matter what, we were going downfield. It felt awfully good."

What felt best for Jerry and his teammates was that

they had made history with their victory over Denver. The 55 points they scored set a Super Bowl record. Joe Montana set a Super Bowl record with 5 touchdown passes and was named the game's Most Valuable Player. The victory also made the 49ers the first team to win back-to-back Super Bowls since the Pittsburgh Steelers had done it in 1978 and 1979.

"To win a game the way we did is an achievement," Jerry says.

It was an achievement that was the result of team-work, sacrifice, and a willingness to accept change. Jerry wasn't always happy that his role with the team was different, but he took his best shots at whatever he was asked to do. That ability would serve him well in coming seasons.

9
Catching Up to the Greats

The 49ers' goal during the 1990 season was to become the first team in NFL history to win three Super Bowls in a row. Their rallying cry was "Threepeat!" (a pun on "repeat"). They took their first step toward doing so in an amazing way, thanks to a heroic effort by Jerry.

The 49ers won their first 10 games in a row and finished the regular season with a 14–2 record, the best in the NFL. The wins didn't come easily, though. Injuries to Roger Craig, John Taylor, and wide receiver Mike Sherrard weakened the offense. Roger missed five games and rushed for only 439 yards that season. When John and Mike got hurt, there were so few players available who could catch the ball that backup quarterback Steve Young was used as a receiver.

Luckily for the 49ers, they still had Jerry. They

counted on him more than ever before, and he didn't let them down.

When Roger missed his first game on October 14 against the Atlanta Falcons, Jerry led the team to a 45–35 win by catching 5 touchdown passes. Only two receivers in NFL history—Bob Shaw of the Chicago Cardinals in 1950 and Kellen Winslow of the San Diego Chargers in 1981—had ever caught as many as 5 in one game. Jerry also set a team record by catching 13 passes. His 225 receiving yards in the game made him the 49ers' all-time career leader in receiving yards with 6,938.

Game after game in that 1990 season, Jerry made plays that kept San Francisco's winning streak alive. For instance:

*Against the Cleveland Browns on October 28, he made a critical catch for a first down. This was during a drive that led to the game-winning field goal with only five seconds left to play. The 49ers won, 20–17.

*Against the Green Bay Packers on November 4, he caught 6 passes for 187 yards. He also scored the touchdown that gave the 49ers a 24–20 win.

*The following week against the Dallas Cowboys, Jerry had 12 receptions for 147 yards and a touchdown. The 49ers won, 24–6.

After that, it got a lot tougher for Jerry. In his next four games, he did not catch any touchdown passes. Only once did he top 100 receiving yards.

The injury to Roger Craig, San Francisco's number one rusher, hurt the 49ers' rushing attack so much that opposing teams expected a pass on almost every play. They knew most of the passes would go to Jerry because the other key receivers were injured, so they smothered him with defensive backs. The Los Angeles Rams used five to cover him in a game on November 25. He still caught seven passes, but the 49ers lost for the first time, 28–17. The next week, the New York

Most Pass Receptions in One Season

108—Sterling Sharpe,
   Green Bay Packers, 1992

106—Art Monk,
   Washington Redskins, 1984

101—Charley Hennigan,
   Houston Oilers, 1964

100—Lionel Taylor,
   Denver Broncos, 1961

100—**Jerry Rice,**
   San Francisco 49ers, 1990

100—Haywood Jeffires,
   Houston Oilers, 1991

Giants held him to one catch for 13 yards, but San Francisco still won, 7–3.

Jerry kept battling through the long, tough season. Teams found they could stop him, but not for long. The next time Jerry faced the Rams, he got revenge with 5 catches for 104 yards. He also scored a 60-yard touchdown. The 49ers won, 26–10.

Jerry finished the regular season as the league leader in receiving yards (1,502) and receptions (100). Only three receivers had ever caught 100 or more passes in a season before.

In the playoffs, Jerry joined another great receiver in the record book. From 1974 to 1987, John Stallworth of the Pittsburgh Steelers caught 12 touchdown passes in post-season games, the most by any receiver in NFL history. Jerry tied John's record in a game against the Redskins on January 12, 1991.

Jerry's record-tying catch was a beauty. The Redskins were leading, 10–7, early in the second quarter. The 49ers had the ball on Washington's 10-yard line. Joe Montana took the snap and scrambled around avoiding tacklers as he waited for a receiver to get open. Joe looked at Jerry three times. Then he fired the ball. The pass was high, but Jerry caught it with his fingertips for a touchdown. The 49ers went on to win, 28–10.

The victory over the Redskins sent the 49ers to the NFC championship game. All they needed to do was beat the Giants at San Francisco's Candlestick Park and they would return to the Super Bowl. Their goal was in sight.

The game was hard-fought and intense. Defense ruled the day. Jerry caught 5 passes for 54 yards, and John Taylor scored the game's only touchdown. All the other points were scored by field goals.

The 49ers were leading, 13-12, with about two minutes and 40 seconds left to play. They had the ball on the Giants' 43-yard line when Roger Craig took a handoff. Roger charged into the line, where he was hit by Giants nose tackle Erik Howard. Suddenly, the ball popped loose and flew in the air. It came down in the hands of linebacker Lawrence Taylor. The Giants had recovered the fumble.

The crowd of 66,334 fans watched anxiously as the Giants began moving the ball. Five plays later, they were on the 49ers' 25-yard line with only four seconds left to play. New York called a timeout and then lined up for a field goal.

Jerry and his teammates on the 49ers' offense stood on the sideline and prayed the Giants would miss. The crowd was hushed. The 49ers' dream of a third trip to the Super Bowl was on the line.

Placekicker Matt Bahr booted the ball. The kick was up, but the ball started to fade to the left. It looked like it was going to miss, but it didn't. The kick was good. The Giants had won, 15–13.

The loss was heartbreaking for the 49ers and their fans. After the game, Giants defensive back Mark Collins told reporters he could see how much Jerry had wanted to win. "I kept moving around, staring at his eyes," Collins said. "That's the way I play everybody. You look into their eyes and you can see if they've come to play. Rice came to play."

The loss to the Giants turned out to be the last hurrah for Jerry and some of the teammates he had played with for six seasons. The following spring, Roger Craig and Ronnie Lott left the 49ers to play for the Raiders.

On July 27, 1991, Jerry welcomed a new person into his life: a son, Jerry Jr. The new baby was the high point of Jerry's summer. In August, he learned that Joe Montana would be out for a while because of an elbow injury. Joe ended up being operated on in October and, in fact, didn't play again until the final game of the 1992 season.

Jerry missed Joe very much back in 1991. The 49ers' quarterback during that season was Steve Young. Steve is a fine all-around athlete, but he and Jerry did not have the kind of chemistry that Joe and Jerry did.

It took Jerry a while to get used to playing with Steve. Unlike Joe, Steve liked to run with the ball when he saw that his receivers were covered. Joe was more patient. He knew that if he waited long enough, Jerry would get open.

Steve did not throw to Jerry as often as Jerry liked. In their first eight games together in 1991, Jerry averaged only 4 catches per game. Against the Los Angeles Raiders on September 29, Jerry caught only 3 passes for 38 yards. Against the Philadelphia Eagles on October 27, he caught only 2 for 4 yards. But somehow, Jerry was still able to lead the team in receptions (80), receiving yards (1,206), and touchdowns (14) that season.

It was a tough season. The 49ers weren't as good as they had been in the past. Jerry was their biggest threat on offense, and opposing teams covered him with three defensive backs in almost every game. Steve got hurt in November and missed all or parts of seven games. Backup quarterback Steve Bono filled in, and Jerry had to get used to yet another quarterback.

The 49ers ended the 1991 season with a 10–6 record and missed the playoffs for the first time since 1982. There were, however, a few bright moments for Jerry. Against the Seattle Seahawks on December 8, he caught six passes and became the 49ers' all-time leader in career receptions with 514. He also caught a touchdown pass in the game. It was the 89th scoring reception of his career. Only two receivers in NFL history had more: Steve Largent of the Seahawks (100) and Don Hutson of the Packers (99).

After the season, Jerry asked the 49ers for a new contract. He wanted $16 million to play for them for the next four years. The 49ers said they would pay him $10 million. Jerry decided that wasn't enough, so he didn't show up for training camp in July 1992.

"I've had seven good years in this league," Jerry told

reporters. "No matter what category you look at in stats or ability, I'm near the top of the list. I don't want to brag about my stats, but one thing I can say is if the 49ers give me this contract, I'm going to get better and make the team better. That's a promise."

For a couple of weeks, San Francisco fans were scared that Jerry might not play at all that season. It was also possible that he would be traded, but Jerry didn't really want to leave the team. "In a way, I could never see myself in another uniform," he said. "The fans in San Francisco are great, the best in the league. I have played with some great players, but you have to leave the possibility open that I could leave the team. It's a business. It's nothing personal."

Two weeks before the first game of the season, Jerry got a new contract from the 49ers. The team agreed to pay him almost $8 million during the next three seasons. It wasn't quite what Jerry wanted, but it was enough to get him to live up to his promise.

The 49ers returned to their old, awesome form. Their offense was the best in the league. They finished the regular season with a 14–2 record and made it all the way to the NFC championship game. Jerry again led the team in receptions (84), receiving yards (1,201), and touchdowns (10).

Jerry felt more comfortable playing with Steve Young, but there were times when he still complained. "I wasn't getting the ball much early in the season and if it had happened a few years ago, I would have gone completely off," he told reporters. "I've grown a lot. This season, Steve and I are growing together."

Steve didn't mind it when Jerry returned to the huddle and said after almost every play, "Get me the ball!"

"I love it, because he wants the ball," Steve says. "That's him. That's why he's going to the Hall of Fame."

That's also why Jerry holds so many records. On December 6, 1992, against the Miami Dolphins, he broke Steve Largent's all-time record of 100 career touchdown catches. The 49ers had the ball on the Dolphins' 12-yard line with about nine minutes left to play in the game. Jerry cut quickly and caught the pass right in the middle of the field. He sprinted into the end zone, where he was mobbed by his teammates. Then he held the ball over his head and ran off the field as the crowd in Candlestick Park cheered wildly.

"I've been chasing this for a long, long time," he told reporters after the game.

Jerry nabbed one more important record before he was done for the season. In the NFC championship game against the Cowboys, he caught a 5-yard touchdown pass that made him the NFL's all-time leader in post-season scoring receptions. It was the 13th touchdown he had scored in post-season play. Not bad for a guy who didn't score any in playoff games during his first three seasons in the league.

The 49ers lost the game, 30–20, but the season had still been a great success. The team had rebounded from the disappointment of 1991, and the future looked bright. Although Joe Montana had only played in the last game of the season due to his injury, replacement Steve Young was named the NFL's Most Valuable Player for 1992. This led to changes, however. Joe didn't want to sit on the bench behind Steve in the future, so he asked to be traded. In April 1993, Joe was traded to the Kansas City Chiefs to take the starting quarterback job.

Although it would be the last season in which Jerry played with Joe, for Jerry, 1992 was the season in which "I've kind of kicked myself in gear for the second half of my career."

The second half begins in 1993. You can bet that when it's over, the NFL record book will be stuffed with Rice.

10 Hands on the Record Book

When Jerry was in high school, college recruiters and coaches thought he was too slow. When he was in college, pro scouts and coaches thought he was too slow. One thing he *wasn't* slow about was proving them wrong.

It took him eight seasons to become the NFL's all-time leader in touchdown receptions. Steve Largent of the Seattle Seahawks, the former leader, set the old record in 14 seasons. In 10 games over 6 seasons, Jerry tied the NFL record for most touchdown catches in post-season play (12). He broke the record in 12 games in his 8th season. John Stallworth of the Pittsburgh Steelers needed 18 games over 14 seasons to set the old record.

In 1991, when he was 29 years old, Jerry became the youngest player ever to catch 500 passes in a career. He is already the 49ers' all-time leader in receptions with 610, receiving yards with 10,273, and touch-downs with 103.

Jerry has said that he wants to play until at least 1998. If he does, he will certainly become the NFL's all-time leader in receptions and receiving yards. After the 1992 season, he ranked ninth in receptions and eighth in receiving yards. "I want to get every record in the book that a receiver can," he says.

There's no reason to think he can't. He keeps himself in top physical shape and has yet to miss a game because of injury. "Receivers get beat up and they miss games, but not Jerry," says Tim Rooney, director of pro personnel for the New York Giants. "He's played every game. Every game he plays is a big game because other teams get up to play him and the 49ers. And his performance never drops off."

"Beyond his natural athletic ability is an inner drive and commitment to being the best," says Coach Seifert. "He enjoys the inner feelings he gets from being the classiest receiver, from the way he carries himself to the way he goes out and catches the football."

"Jerry's stamina is another thing to consider," says Bill Walsh. "He's just as fresh and dangerous in the fourth quarter as he is in the first, or just as fresh in the tenth game of the season as he is in the first game."

"The thing I admire most about Jerry is the way he works," says former 49ers defensive back Dave Waymer. "Sometimes when a guy is successful, there's a tendency to get complacent. With Jerry, there's no complacency anywhere."

The key to Jerry's success has always been his willingness to work hard. "People think that I'm a natural receiver, like I was born with everything I've got," he says. "But everything that I've achieved, I've worked at. There are so many receivers out there with good hands, that are fast, but they don't have that work ethic or determination to be the best. If you want to be the best, you have to work at it."

Early in his career, Jerry learned some tough but valuable lessons about what it takes to succeed as a pro athlete. At first, he was confused when he struggled as a rookie. "Everything had come so easy for me," he says. "I thought I knew it all." He found out, however, that talent and hard work aren't always enough. He had to study and make sacrifices. For instance, he had to devote more of his spare time to studying playbooks.

Perhaps the toughest lesson Jerry learned was how to deal with criticism. He heard a lot of boos his rookie season. He made it through the rough times because he believed in himself. "You've got to believe in yourself or no one else will," he says.

Jerry's firm belief in himself is summed up best by a line about him in the 1992 49ers Media Guide, a booklet that tells reporters about the team: "Pressure performer who wants the ball when the game is on the line."

Jerry in the 1990's
*Led the NFL in receptions (100) and receiving yards (1,502) in 1990.
*Tied an NFL record with five touchdown catches in one game on October 14, 1990, against the Falcons.
*Became the NFL all-time touchdown reception leader (103) in 1992.
*Broke the NFL record for most career touchdown catches in post-season play in 1993.
*Played in the Pro Bowl in 1990, 1991, 1992, and 1993.
*Named All-Pro in 1990 and 1992.

That desire is the reason why Jerry has complained sometimes about not having enough passes thrown to him. He says the complaints are not because he wants more glory. He wants the ball because he wants to win. "I don't believe I've handled things that way," he says. "I just want to win very badly. With all the success, I'm still the same old person. I'm not the cocky type. I'm not conceited. I know what it's going to take for me to get better each year. I've got to work hard. And I'm always going to be down to earth."

"He has matured so much," says 49ers center Jesse Sapolu. "You don't see him on national TV now talking about not catching as many touchdowns or complaining about something else. Jerry has always had his teammates' respect as a superstar. Now he has it not only as a superstar, but as a team leader. That is a big difference. We can see that inner peace starting to build within him."

"I'm more at peace with myself," Jerry agrees. "There are things I cannot control that are solely up to the coaches and the quarterback. I'm more at peace with all of that."

Jerry's goal is to be the best receiver ever to play pro football. He does admit, however, that "I'm not there right now. I really don't like to overrate myself. I'll let others give me compliments. If they want to compliment me, fine. But I don't want to be conceited and say that myself. I wouldn't want to say that I'm the best receiver in football or anything like that. That just wouldn't be right."

There are plenty of people who *are* willing to say it for him. "The first time I saw him, he was the best I ever saw," says Dwight Clark, Jerry's former teammate on the 49ers. "Jerry's like a Michael Jordan, a Joe Montana. He's a step above the rest."

"I haven't ever worked with a wide receiver with greater ability than Jerry Rice," Bill Walsh says. "There is no better player at his position in the game. He studies the game, he's tough, he concentrates, and has tremendous athletic ability."

Steve Sabol is the president of NFL Films. His company produces videos of sports highlights and bloopers. He has watched thousands of game films and seen the all-time greats in action. Steve says, "Jerry is the greatest receiver ever to play the game. It's a terrible thing for a film historian to say. We're supposed to always be looking at the past. But I've seen it all, and Rice is the greatest receiver to ever play the game. He's complete in everything. Other receivers might be better in one area than Rice, but they're not as complete."

There is no doubt that one day Jerry will be elected to the Pro Football Hall of Fame. It is one of his biggest goals. But through all his success and records and honors, Jerry has never forgotten what sports are really all about.

"I want to be in the Hall of Fame with guys who didn't play for the money as much as for the challenge," Jerry says. "I really try not to focus on the records. I'm just like a little kid on the field. The fun is still in the game for me."